INTRODUCTION

The Dalai Lama is a spiritual leader and political figure   who is revered as the head of the Tibetan Buddhist tradition. He is believed to be the reincarnation of Avalokiteshvara, the bodhisattva of compassion. The title "Dalai Lama" translates to "ocean of wisdom" in Tibetan.

The current Dalai Lama is Tenzin Gyatso, who was born on July 6, 1935, in Tibet. He was recognized as the 14th Dalai Lama at the age of two and was officially enthroned as the spiritual leader of Tibet at the age of four. He has been a prominent figure in advocating for Tibet's autonomy and human rights, as well as promoting peace, compassion, and interfaith harmony.

The Dalai Lama has received numerous awards and honors for his efforts in promoting peace, including the Nobel Peace Prize in 1989. He has also written numerous books on Buddhism, spirituality, and global issues. His teachings and quotes are widely respected and followed by people of various faiths and backgrounds around the world.

In addition to his spiritual leadership, the Dalai Lama has also been engaged in efforts to promote environmental conservation, gender equality, and education, among other causes. He has traveled extensively and met with world leaders, religious figures, and ordinary people to spread his message of compassion, peace, and understanding.

One of the Dalai Lama's key teachings is the promotion of compassion towards all beings. He advocates for the practice of loving-kindness and empathy towards others, regardless of their background, culture, or beliefs. He often emphasizes the need for understanding and tolerance, as well as the importance of forgiveness and reconciliation in resolving conflicts and promoting harmonious relationships.

In addition to his teachings, the Dalai Lama is known for his warm and humble personality, as well as his sense of humor. He has a genuine and approachable demeanor, and he often engages in dialogues and interactions with people from all walks of life, regardless of their beliefs or background.

It's worth noting that the Dalai Lama's teachings and his approach to leadership have inspired millions of people worldwide, transcending religious, cultural, and political boundaries. His message of compassion, mindfulness, and ethics continues to have a profound impact on individuals, communities, and the world at large.

A disciplined mind leads to happiness, and an undisciplined mind leads to suffering.

- Dalai Lama

A truly compassionate
attitude toward others does not
change even if they behave
negatively or hurt you.

- Dalai Lama

All suffering is caused by ignorance. People inflict pain on others in the selfish pursuit of their own happiness or satisfaction.

\- Dalai Lama

Anger is the ultimate destroyer
of your own peace of mind.

- Dalai Lama

As you breathe in, cherish
yourself. As you breathe out,
cherish all Beings.

- Dalai Lama

Be kind whenever possible.
It is always possible.

- Dalai Lama

Because of lack of moral principle, human life becomes worthless. Moral principle, truthfulness, is a key factor. If we lose that, then there is no future.

- Dalai Lama

Calm mind brings inner
strength and self-confidence, so
that's very important for
good health.

- Dalai Lama

Choose to be optimistic,
it feels better.

- Dalai Lama

Compassion is not religious business, it is human business, it is not luxury, it is essential for our own peace and mental stability, it is essential for human survival.

- Dalai Lama

Death means change our
clothes. Clothes become old, then
time to come change. So, this
body become old, and then time
come, take young body.

- Dalai Lama

Do not let the behavior of others
destroy your inner peace.

- Dalai Lama

Don't ever mistake my
silence for ignorance, my
calmness for acceptance or my
kindness for weakness.
Compassion and tolerance are
not a sign of weakness, but a sign
of strength.

- Dalai Lama

Even an animal, if you show
genuine affection, gradually trust
develops... If you always showing
bad face and beating, how can
you develop friendship?

- Dalai Lama

Even when we have
physical hardships, we can be
very happy.

- Dalai Lama

Every day, think as you wake up, today I am fortunate to be alive, I have a precious human life, I am not going to waste it. I am going to use all my energies to develop myself, to expand my heart out to others; to achieve enlightenment for the benefit of all beings. I am going to have kind thoughts towards others, I am not going to get angry or think badly about others. I am going to benefit others as much as I can.

- Dalai Lama

Everyone wants a happy life
without difficulties or suffering.
We create many of the problems
we face. No one intentionally
creates problems, but we tend to
be slaves to powerful emotions
like anger, hatred and attachment
that are based on misconceived
projections about people and
things. We need to find ways of
reducing these emotions by
eliminating the ignorance that
underlies them and applying
opposing forces.

- Dalai Lama

Follow the three R's:
– Respect for self.
– Respect for others.
– Responsibility for all your
actions.

- Dalai Lama

Forget the failures. Keep the lessons.

- Dalai Lama

Generally speaking, if a human being never shows anger, then I think something's wrong. He's not right in the brain.

- Dalai Lama

Give the ones you love wings
to fly, roots to come back and
reasons to stay.

- Dalai Lama

Happiness doesn't always
come from a pursuit. Sometimes
it comes when we least
expect it.

- Dalai Lama

Happiness is not something readymade. It comes from your own actions.

- Dalai Lama

Hard times build determination
and inner strength. Through them
we can also come to appreciate
the uselessness of anger. Instead
of getting angry nurture a deep
caring and respect for
troublemakers because by
creating such trying
circumstances they provide us
with invaluable opportunities to
practice tolerance and patience.

- Dalai Lama

Home is where you feel at
home and are treated well.

- Dalai Lama

I believe compassion to be one
of the few things we can practice
that will bring immediate and
long-term happiness to our lives.
I'm not talking about the short-
term gratification of pleasures
like sex, drugs or gambling
(though I'm not knocking them),
but something that will bring true
and lasting happiness. The kind
that sticks.

- Dalai Lama

I believe the very purpose of
our life is to seek happiness.
Whether one believes in religion
or not, whether one believes in
that religion or this religion, we
are all seeking something better
in life. So, I think, the very motion
of our life is towards happiness.

- Dalai Lama

I defeat my enemies when
I make them my friends.

- Dalai Lama

I find hope in the darkest of
days, and focus in the brightest.
I do not judge the universe.

- Dalai Lama

If a problem is fixable, if a situation is such that you can do something about it, then there is no need to worry. If it's not fixable, then there is no help in worrying. There is no benefit in worrying whatsoever.

- Dalai Lama

If it can be solved, there's no
need to worry, and if it can't be
solved, worry is of no use.

- Dalai Lama

If someone has a gun and is trying to kill you, it would be reasonable to shoot back with your own gun.

- Dalai Lama

If you can cultivate the right attitude, your enemies are your best spiritual teachers because their presence provides you with the opportunity to enhance and develop tolerance, patience and understanding.

- Dalai Lama

If you don't love yourself, you cannot love others. You will not be able to love others. If you have no compassion for yourself then you are not able of developing compassion for others.

- Dalai Lama

If you have a particular faith
or religion, that is good. But you
can survive without it.

- Dalai Lama

If you have peace of mind,
when you meet with problems
and difficulties, they won't disturb
your inner peace. You'll be able
to employ your human
intelligence more effectively. But,
if your mental state is disturbed,
full of emotion, it is very difficult
to cope with problems, because
the mind that is full of emotion is
biased, unable to see reality. So,
whatever you do will be
unrealistic and naturally fail.

- Dalai Lama

If you think you are too small to
make a difference, try sleeping
with a mosquito.

- Dalai Lama

If you want others to be happy,
practice compassion. If you want
to be happy, practice
compassion.

- Dalai Lama

If your heart has peace,
nothing can disturb you.

- Dalai Lama

In order to become prosperous,
a person must initially work very
hard, so he or she has to sacrifice
a lot of leisure time.

- Dalai Lama

In order to carry a positive
action, we must develop here a
positive vision.

- Dalai Lama

In our struggle for freedom, truth
is the only weapon we possess.

- Dalai Lama

In the practice of tolerance,
one's enemy is the best teacher.

- Dalai Lama

Inner peace is the key: if you have inner peace, the external problems do not affect your deep sense of peace and tranquility... without this inner peace, no matter how comfortable your life is materially, you may still be worried, disturbed, or unhappy because of circumstances.

- Dalai Lama

Instead of wondering
WHY this is happening to you,
consider why this is happening
to YOU.

- Dalai Lama

It is very important to generate a good attitude, a good heart, as much as possible. From this, happiness in both the short term and the long term for both yourself and others will come.

- Dalai Lama

Judge your success
by what you had to give up in
order to get it.

- Dalai Lama

Just one small positive
thought in the morning can
change your whole day.

- Dalai Lama

Look at situations
from all angles, and you will
become more open.

- Dalai Lama

Love and compassion are
necessities, not luxuries. Without
them humanity cannot survive.

- Dalai Lama

Love is the absence of judgment.

- Dalai Lama

More compassionate mind,
more sense of concern for other's
well-being, is source of
happiness.

- Dalai Lama

My faith helps me overcome
such negative emotions and find
my equilibrium.

- Dalai Lama

My religion is very simple.
My religion is kindness.

- Dalai Lama

Neither a space station nor an enlightened mind can be realized in a day.

- Dalai Lama

Never give up.
No matter what is happening, no
matter what is going on around
you, never give up.

- Dalai Lama

Old friends pass away, new
friends appear. It is just like the
days. An old day passes, a new
day arrives. The important thing
is to make it meaningful: a
meaningful friend – or a
meaningful day.

- Dalai Lama

Only the development of
compassion and understanding
for others can bring us the
tranquility and happiness we all
seek.

- Dalai Lama

Our prime purpose
in this life is to help others. And if
you can't help them, at least don't
hurt them.

- Dalai Lama

Pain can change you, but that doesn't mean it has to be a bad change. Take that pain and turn it into wisdom.

- Dalai Lama

People take different roads
seeking fulfillment and happiness.
Just because they're not on your
road doesn't mean they've gotten
lost.

- Dalai Lama

Remember that silence is
sometimes the best answer.

- Dalai Lama

Remember that sometimes not
getting what you want is a
wonderful stroke of luck.

- Dalai Lama

Remember that the best
relationship is one in which your
love for each other exceeds your
need for each other.

- Dalai Lama

Share your knowledge.
It is a way to achieve
immortality.

- Dalai Lama

Silence is sometimes the best
answer.

- Dalai Lama

Sleep is the best meditation.

- Dalai Lama

Smile if you want a smile from
another face.

- Dalai Lama

Some mischievous people
always there. Last several
thousand years, always there. In
future, also.

- Dalai Lama

Someone else's action should not determine your response.

- Dalai Lama

Sometimes one creates a
dynamic impression by saying
something, and sometimes one
creates as significant an
impression by remaining silent.

- Dalai Lama

Take into account
that great love and great
achievements involve
great risk.

- Dalai Lama

The best way to resolve any
problem in the human world is
for all sides to sit down and talk.

- Dalai Lama

The creatures that inhabit
this earth-be they human beings
or animals-are here to
contribute, each in its own
particular way, to the beauty and
prosperity of the world.

- Dalai Lama

The goal is not to be
better than the other man, but
your previous self.

- Dalai Lama

The important thing is that men should have a purpose in life. It should be something useful, something good.

- Dalai Lama

The period of greatest gain in
knowledge and experience is the
most difficult period in one's life.

- Dalai Lama

The planet does not need
more successful people.
The planet desperately needs
more peacemakers, healers,
restorers, storytellers, and lovers
of all kinds.

- Dalai Lama

The purpose of our lives is
to be happy.

- Dalai Lama

The topic of compassion
is not at all religious business; it is
important to know it is human
business, it is a question of human
survival.

- Dalai Lama

The true hero is one who conquers his own anger and hatred.

- Dalai Lama

······ 82 ·····

The ultimate source of happiness
is not money and power, but
warm-heartedness.

- Dalai Lama

The ultimate source of my mental
happiness is my peace of mind.
Nothing can destroy this except
my own anger.

- Dalai Lama

The way to change others' minds
is with affection, and not anger.

- Dalai Lama

The whole purpose of religion
is to facilitate love and
compassion, patience, tolerance,
humility, and forgiveness.

- Dalai Lama

There are only two days in the
year that nothing can be done.
One is called yesterday and the
other is called tomorrow. Today
is the right day to love, believe, do
and mostly live.

- Dalai Lama

There is a saying in Tibetan,
'Tragedy should be utilized as a
source of strength.' No matter
what sort of difficulties, how
painful experience is, if we lose
our hope, that's our real disaster.

- Dalai Lama

This is my simple religion.
There is no need for temples; no
need for complicated philosophy.
Our own brain, our own heart is
our temple; the philosophy is
kindness.

- Dalai Lama

Through difficult experiences,
life sometimes becomes more
meaningful.

- Dalai Lama

Time passes unhindered.
When we make mistakes, we
cannot turn the clock back and
try again. All we can do is use the
present well.

- Dalai Lama

To conquer oneself is a
greater victory than to conquer
thousands in a battle.

- Dalai Lama

To remain indifferent to the challenges we face is indefensible. If the goal is noble, whether or not it is realized within our lifetime is largely irrelevant. What we must do therefore is to strive and persevere and never give up.

- Dalai Lama

Too much self-centered attitude,
you see, brings, you see, isolation.
Result: loneliness, fear, anger.
The extreme self-centered
attitude is the source of suffering.

- Dalai Lama

True friendship develops not as a result of money or power but on the basis of genuine human affection.

- Dalai Lama

True happiness comes from
having a sense of inner peace and
contentment, which in turn must
be achieved by cultivating
altruism, love and compassion,
and by eliminating anger,
selfishness and greed.

- Dalai Lama

We all have to live together,
so we might as well live together
happily.

- Dalai Lama

We can live without religion and
meditation, but we cannot survive
without human affection.

- Dalai Lama

We can never obtain peace
in the outer world until we make
peace with ourselves.

- Dalai Lama

When reason ends, then anger
begins. Therefore, anger is a sign
of weakness.

- Dalai Lama

When we are caught up in a
destructive emotion, we lose one
of our greatest assets: our
independence.

- Dalai Lama

When we are motivated by
compassion and wisdom, the
results of our actions benefit
everyone, not just our individual
selves or some immediate
convenience. When we are able
to recognize and forgive ignorant
actions of the past, we gain
strength to constructively solve
the problems of the present.

- Dalai Lama

When we feel love and kindness
toward others, it not only makes
others feel loved and cared for,
but it helps us also to develop
inner happiness and peace.

- Dalai Lama

When we meet real tragedy in
life, we can react in two ways–
either by losing hope and falling
into self-destructive habits, or by
using the challenge to find our
inner strength.

- Dalai Lama

When you practice gratefulness,
there is a sense of respect
toward others.

- Dalai Lama

When you realize you've made
a mistake, take immediate steps
to correct it.

- Dalai Lama

When you talk you are only
repeating something you already
know. But if you listen you may
learn something new.

- Dalai Lama

Whether one is rich or poor, educated or illiterate, religious or non-believing, man or woman, black, white, or brown, we are all the same. Physically, emotionally, and mentally, we are all equal. We all share basic needs for food, shelter, safety, and love. We all aspire to happiness and we all shun suffering. Each of us has hopes, worries, fears, and dreams. Each of us wants the best for our family and loved ones. We all experience pain when we suffer loss and joy when we achieve what we seek. On this fundamental level, religion, ethnicity, culture, and language make no difference.

- Dalai Lama

World peace must develop from inner peace. Peace is not just mere absence of violence. Peace is, I think, the manifestation of human compassion.

- Dalai Lama

You have to start giving first and
expect absolutely nothing.

- Dalai Lama

Printed in Great Britain
by Amazon

58262808R00066